IS YOUR CITY HEADING FOR FINANCIAL DIFFICULTY:

A GUIDEBOOK FOR SMALL CITIES AND OTHER GOVERNMENTAL UNITS

SMALL CITIES FINANCIAL MANAGEMENT PROJECT:

Prepared By
Project Director: Philip Rosenberg
Principal Contributor: C. Wayne Stallings

MUNICIPAL FINANCE OFFICERS ASSOCIATION of U.S. and Canada.
In Conjunction With
PEAT, MARWICK, MITCHELL & CO.
INSTITUTE OF GOVERNMENT, UNIVERSITY OF GEORGIA

i

This book was prepared with the support of the National Science Foundation Grant APR76-19208. However, any opinions, conclusions, and/or recommendations herein are those of the authors and do not necessarily reflect the views of the National Science Foundation.

FOREWORD

The magnitude and severity of the fiscal crisis of major municipalities has eclipsed the problems of smaller governmental units. Although their problems are perhaps not as dramatic; they too are encountering increased pressure on available resources which is forcing them to review and revise their existing financial management systems.

Many advancements in financial management policies and procedures have been made in the context of the needs of larger governmental units. Officials in smaller units of government may recognize the problems in achieving sound financial management. However, they are often unaware of the methods required to solve them or the resources available to address the need.

In the past, only components and supporting techniques of sophisticated approaches have been applicable to small city needs, and then only if translated and simplified. Little has been done nationally to adjust financial management approaches to the needs of smaller units of government. The Municipal Finance Officers Association has addressed this problem through the publication of this guidebook, a guidebook to improved financial management, and handbooks in budgeting, capital programming, accounting, debt management, and treasury management. Each publication presents innovative financial management policies and procedures tailored to meet the needs of smaller units of government.

Is Your City Heading for Financial Difficulty? A Guidebook for Small Cities and Other Governmental Units presents a set of techniques a municipality may use to perform a thorough analysis of its financial condition. The methods of analysis are presented in a simple, step-by-step, format.

This project was funded by a grant from the National Science Foundation. The Municipal Finance Officers Association wishes to thank the public officials from Alabama, California, Georgia, Illinois, Massachusetts, Oregon, South Carolina and Tennessee who provided review and comment on the documents in a series of workshops. We wish to thank the members of the Project Advisory Panel for their significant investment of time and energy in every phase of our work: Martin A. Anochie, Jo Ann Davidson, Dennis Dycus, Betty Jo Harker, Alvin J. Keller, Anthony T. Logalbo, John Matzer, Jr., and William E. Watkins. In addition, we wish to thank our two sub-contractors: The Institute of Government of the University of Georgia, and Peat, Marwick, Mitchell & Co. A special note of thanks goes to Charles K. Coe of the Institute for his valuable contribution in the preparation of each publication. Among the staff of the Municipal Finance Officers Association, the following individuals provided valuable assistance during the project: Eileen Briesch, Marcia Claxton, Dick Haas, Phyllis Myerson, Rebecca Russum, James Williams, and Joe Ziemba. Finally, we wish to thank Dr. Trudi Miller, NSF Program Manager, for her support during the project.

Donald W. Beatty
Executive Director
Municipal Finance Officers Association
Chicago, Illinois

CONTENTS

Chapter Four:
A Large Amount of Current Costs Are Being Deferred to the Future

Chapter Five:
Use of Unsound Financial Management Practices

Part II. Procedures for Developing and Maintaining the Trends

Exhibits:

Appendix

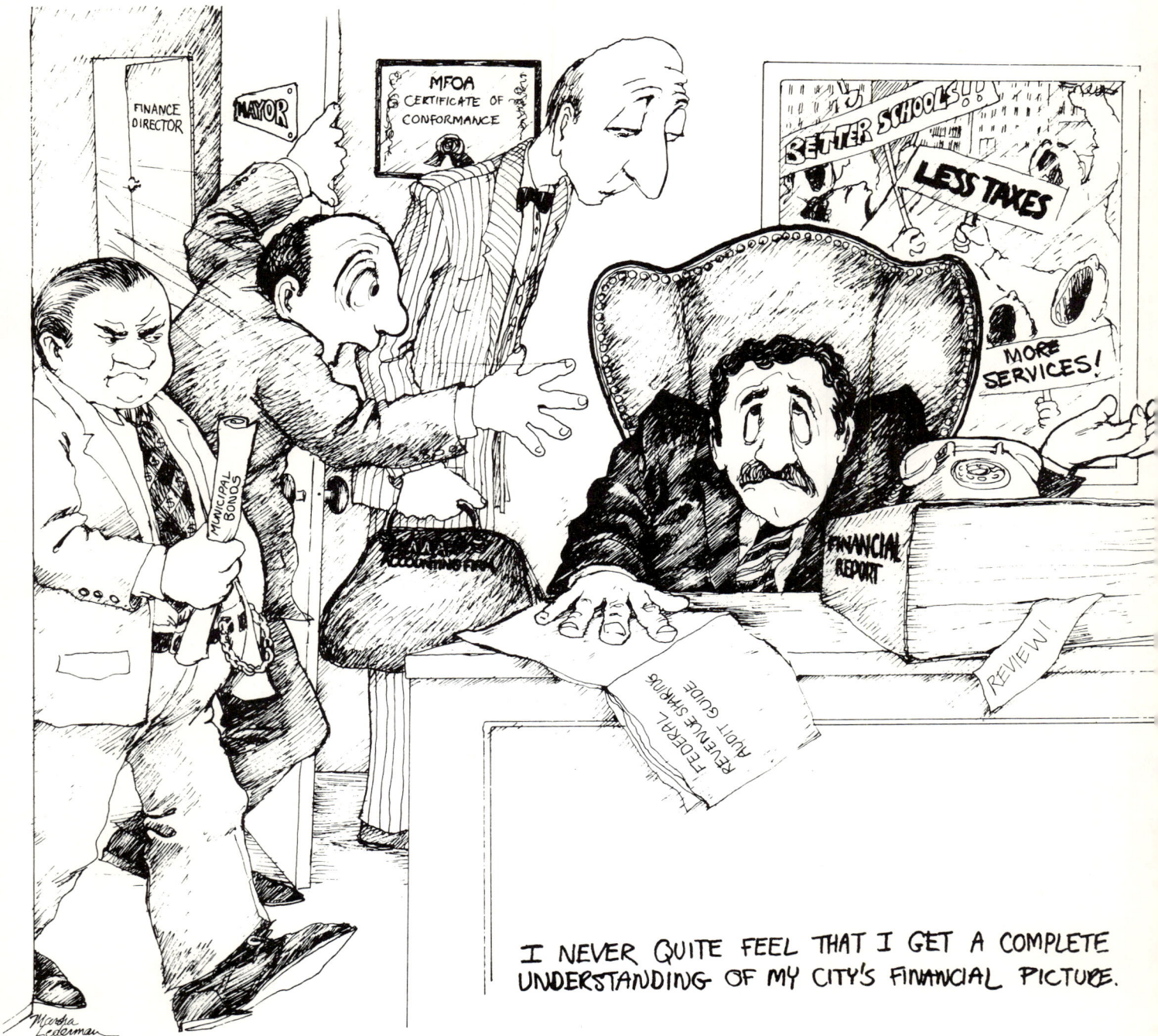

I NEVER QUITE FEEL THAT I GET A COMPLETE UNDERSTANDING OF MY CITY'S FINANCIAL PICTURE.

Introduction

Is your municipality headed for financial trouble? In the wake of the recent fiscal crises faced by large cities, municipal officials from larger cities and smaller towns across the country are asking themselves this question. It is often difficult for local officals to get a complete picture of their financial situation.

Several factors make it difficult for municipal officials in smaller units of government to perform a thorough analysis of municipal financial condition.

- There are few standards against which municipal finances can be measured with confidence.

- It is not easy to compare one city to another because of the differences which exist in city populations, services provided, and legal requirements.

- It is difficult to measure factors external to the city government itself (political, economic, and social forces) which have a strong influence on financial well being.

- The problems which create fiscal difficulties seldom emerge overnight; rather, they develop slowly, thus making potential difficulties less obvious.

- The information needed to assess problems is seldom readily available in a useable format.

This guidebook presents a set of techniques which a municipality can use to perform an analysis of its municipal financial condition. The approach suggested here seeks to overcome some of the difficulties just cited.

- It allows municipal officials to focus on trends within their city without calling for comparisons to externally developed standards or to conditions in other cities.

- It focuses attention on factors and trends over a relatively long period of time, thus allowing municipal officials to see whether possible problems are intensifying or improving.

- It provides a framework for assembling and analyzing information about the city on a regular basis.

This approach relies heavily on the determination and analysis of selected key trends. The identification of one of these trends, however, does not automatically point to fiscal decline. Some trends, which on the surface appear adverse, may, after careful analysis, prove harmless. Moreover, the techniques presented in this guidebook are intended to provide an overview of the financial condition of a municipality. The results obtained from using these techniques are a good beginning point for analysis, not a conclusion.

In addition, these techniques are simple to implement if your municipality follows reasonably good accounting and financial reporting procedures.

The following sections describe the techniques you can use to analyze your municipal financial condition. Part I describes the conditions which contribute to municipal financial difficulty. A brief general discussion of each condition is presented on the white pages included in Part I. Then a more detailed discussion of the key indicators or trends which are associated with each condition are presented on the yellow pages following each general discussion. Part II presents detailed procedures which may be regularly followed to collect the data and to measure and analyze the trends which are associated with each condition.

PART I
Conditions Contributing to Fiscal Decline

Obviously, there are many factors which can cause fiscal problems for a municipality. This guidebook focuses on five major factors which appear most significant:

1. the economic vitality of the municipality is declining;

2. municipal financial independence is being lost;

3. municipal productivity is declining;

4. a large amount of current municipal costs are being deferred or postponed to the future; and,

5. financial management practices of the municipality are ineffective.

Each of the following chapters provides a brief description of these factors and their significance. In addition, specific contributing trends or indicators are presented. Each of these trends is assigned a number which appears in ( ) for identification purposes. A detailed discussion of each of the numbered trends is presented in the yellow pages immediately following the description of each factor.

CHAPTER ONE
Economic Vitality
Is Declining

No municipality can avoid fiscal difficulty over the long run if its economic vitality is deteriorating. A strong economy:

- produces the revenue to support services; and

- creates a positive community environment which attracts residents and businesses.

Moreover, when the economy is strong, the need to expend public funds on such services as police protection, social services, and housing rehabilitation is often less intense. The following specific trends may indicate that the economic vitality of the community is declining.

- Appraised value of real estate per capita in the community is growing too slowly or declining. *(1)*

- Number and value of building permits is declining or growing too slowly. *(2)*

- Number and value of business licenses is declining. *(3)*

- Retail sales are declining or growing at a slower pace. *(4)*

- Expenditures for police and social services are growing as a percent of total expenditures. *(5)*

- Total population is declining. *(6)*

- Income per capita is declining. *(7)*

If several of the above trends are found in your municipality, its economic vitality could be declining. A municipality which is experiencing a decline in its economy should act to create a more favorable economic environment.

Trends *(1) - (7)* are described more fully in the following yellow pages.

TREND ONE
Appraised Value of Real Estate Per Capita Declining

This trend is measured by taking the assessed value of real estate in the community, dividing it by the assessment ratio, and then dividing it again by the population of the community. The following formula may be used:

$$\frac{\text{ASSESSED VALUE} \div \text{ASSESSMENT RATIO}}{\text{MUNICIPAL POPULATION}}$$

This indicator should be computed for each of the past five years. A declining trend could mean one of several things:

- real estate assessment procedures may not be keeping assessed values at the level of fair market values (see Trend 23);

- large tracts of real estate have been removed from the tax base pending redevelopment, making the decline temporary; or,

- large amounts of real estate are becoming non-taxable (a possible bad sign).

TREND TWO
Number and Value of Building Permits Declining

This trend is measured simply by recording the aggregate number and dollar value of building permits over the past five years. Building permits tend to be good barometers of economic activity and vitality. If their number and value is declining, four general reasons should be considered:

- the trend reflects a national recession or decline in construction activity;

- no land is available for new development;

- the economic vitality of the municipality is eroding; and

- a rising tax rate is discouraging new development.

If the first of these is applicable, the problem is likely to be short term, and in any case, is beyond local control. The latter three reasons, however, could foster economic difficulty for the community.

TREND THREE

Slowing Growth or Decline in the Number and Value of Business Licenses

This trend is measured by obtaining the dollar value and the number of business licenses issued in the municipality over the past five years.

The trend may result from a nationwide decline in business activity. It may also mean that the economy of the municipality is stagnating. Again, the former problem cannot be solved by the municipality alone. Municipal decision-makers can adopt, however, a variety of fiscal policies which may facilitate improvement in the local economy (see **A Guidebook to Improved Financial Management for Small Cities and Other Governmental Units**).

TREND FOUR

Slowing Growth or Decline in Retail Sales

This trend is measured by dividing sales tax collections by the sales tax rate as follows:

$$\frac{\text{SALES TAX COLLECTIONS}}{\text{SALES TAX RATE}}$$

If your municipality has no sales tax, it may be possible to obtain applicable figures (i.e., collections made within your municipality) from the state government. The indicator should be computed for each of the past five years.

The significance and underlying causes of this trend are similar to those of building permits and building licenses. An unfavorable trend may be caused by a nationwide economic recession or by a decline in the economic vitality of the municipality.

TREND FIVE

Expenditures for Police and Social Services Increasing as a Percent of Total Expenditures

This trend is measured by adding police and social service expenditures and dividing them by total operating expenditures for the past five years, calculated as follows:

$$\frac{\text{POLICE EXPENDITURES} + \text{SOCIAL SERVICE EXPENDITURES}}{\text{TOTAL EXPENDITURES}}$$

The trend could result from several factors:

- major new programs funded by intergovernmental grants have been started;

- police and social services were underfunded previously;

- a recession has created temporary unemployment in the city (the trend will be reversed when business conditions improve);

- the proportion of elderly (over age 65) and youth (under age 20) in the population of the municipality is increasing, thus placing greater demand on the provision of these services;

- middle income residents are being replaced by less affluent groups which require public assistance; or,

- major employers are closing down, thus creating additional unemployment.

You should determine which causes are appropriate to your situation before concluding the trend is adverse.

TREND SIX
Total Population Declining

Measure this trend by assembling population figures for the current year and for several previous years. If your city does not keep this information, it may be available from a state or regional planning agency. A declining population is sometimes indicative of a declining economic base. Among the underlying causes are:

- residents moving elsewhere for work;

- middle and upper income groups moving outside municipal limits to find housing;

- population becoming generally older, while youth move elsewhere to find employment opportunities;

- the economic vitality of the municipality is eroding; and,

- overall population declining in your region.

In any case, the trend means that the economic base may not continue to support municipal expenditures at current levels without some strain. In theory, the demand for some municipal services should decline with population. Experience has shown, however, that service reduction, even under those conditions, is seldom easy.

TREND SEVEN
Income Per Capita Declining

This trend is measured by assembling the per capita income of city residents over the past five years. The figure should be adjusted for inflation, using the Consumer Price Index (CPI) for each year as follows:

PER CAPITA INCOME EACH YEAR
CPI EACH YEAR

Since few smaller municipalities collect or maintain such data, you will probably have to obtain the information from a state agency, a regional planning agency, or from U.S. Census publications.

A declining income per capita may be the result of:

- a temporary national or regional recession; or,

- a local economic decline.

The second condition may lead to long-term fiscal strain for your local government.

CHAPTER TWO
Financial Independence and Flexibility Is Being Lost

A financially sound city typically has sufficient control over its finances to enable it to weather financial problems and emergencies without crisis. In addition, such municipalities usually have the financial flexibility to respond to the need to support critical programs. This flexibility is a by-product of financial independence: it permits a city to control its own destiny.

Your city's financial independence can be lost in several ways:

- becoming overly dependent on volatile outside funding sources with their matching fund and administrative requirements;

- incurring excessive debt which creates heavy demands on future revenues;

- becoming committed to programs whose costs cannot be readily controlled;

- having statutory limits placed on critical revenue sources, such as the property tax rate; or,

- having the state government mandate extensive costs on the municipality.

The following specific trends may indicate that financial independence and flexibility are being lost.

- A growing percentage of expenditures for basic services being funded by intergovernmental grant funds. (8)

- A growing proportion of own source revenues being committed to meet matching fund requirements. (9)

- A growing debt burden. (10)

- A steady pattern of budget overruns in specific programs or departments. (11)

- A rapid increase in fringe benefits for employees. (12)

- Tax rates for key tax sources approaching legal ceilings. (13)

- Growing proportion of total municipal expenditures going to fund mandated costs. (14)

If several of these trends are found in your municipality, you may be losing vital financial independence. Financial policies should be implemented which ensure that the government can control its financial destiny such as:

- bringing funding for basic services under a more reliable funding base;

- reducing the use of debt financing for capital needs;

- solving the problems or changing the administrative techniques which cause consistent budget overruns; and,

• joining in lobbying efforts in the state legislature to remove burdensome tax ceilings or mandated costs.

Trends *(8) - (14)* are described more fully in the following yellow pages.

TREND EIGHT

Growing Percentage of Expenditures for Basic Services Funded from Intergovernmental Grant Funds

You cannot assess this trend through simple arithmetic. An analysis must be made of the sources of funds used for each local service. Next, you must determine what services are basic and what services might be more readily foregone. Finally, the degree to which each intergovernmental revenue is subject to fluctuation also must be determined.

If, after such an analysis, you conclude that an increasing share of local services are being supported by grants, the financial independence of your jurisdiction may be endangered.

TREND NINE

Growing Proportion of Own Source Revenues Committed to Meet Matching Requirements

This trend is measured by dividing the amount of local funds expended to match grant funds by total own source revenues in each year as follows:

AMOUNT OF FUNDS EXPENDED FOR MATCHING GRANTS
TOTAL OWN SOURCE REVENUES

Because few local governments maintain a total figure for such matching expenditures, it will probably be necessary to perform an analysis of municipal expenditure accounts to obtain accurate figures.

The proportion may be growing for the following reasons:

- previous use of grant funds were inadequate and the municipality is moving towards more aggressive grant application and use; and,

- the municipality is overcommitted to grant-funded programs and is losing its financial independence.

Determining which of these causes is more appropriate will be a highly subjective judgement.

TREND TEN

Growing Debt Burden

Several measures are required to assess this trend as follows:

- growing ratio of long-term general obligation (G.O.) indebtedness to assessed property values (or to true market values) calculated as:

$$\frac{\text{G. O. LONG-TERM INDEBTEDNESS}}{\text{ASSESSED OR MARKET VALUE OF REAL ESTATE}}$$

- growing general obligation long-term indebtedness per capita calculated as:

$$\frac{\text{G. O. LONG-TERM INDEBTEDNESS}}{\text{MUNICIPAL POPULATION}}$$

- growing general obligation debt service payments as a percentage of own source revenues calculated as:

$$\frac{\text{DEBT SERVICE PAYMENTS}}{\text{TOTAL OWN SOURCE REVENUES}}$$

These measures should be computed for each of the past five years. If an increasing trend is found, your city may be unduly restricting its future financial flexibility committing too much future revenue to debt repayments. In such a case, it will probably be desirable to curtail capital expenditures funded by general obligation debt to avoid increasing the future burden.

TREND ELEVEN

Steady Pattern of Budget Overruns in Specific Programs or Departments

This trend is measured by dividing year-end expenditures by the original budget for each program or department as follows:

$$\frac{\text{YEAR END EXPENDITURES}}{\text{ORIGINAL BUDGET}}$$

The original budget should be used because it represents the initial estimate of the cost of providing services. Since many local governments routinely adjust budgets to avoid actual overruns, the revised budget may not be as reliable a standard as the original budget.

A ratio from the above formula of one or greater indicates an overrun. If, over the past five years, a program has consistently scored greater than one, and especially if the size of the ratio is increasing, that program's cost may be out of control. An out-of-control program severely limits the future fiscal flexibility of the jurisdiction because an ever-growing proportion of future revenues must be allocated to meet that program's costs. The basic policies underlying the program should be revised to effect better cost control.

The trend may have other causes. Inadequate allowance may have been made in the original budget for inflation, service demands, salary adjustments, or retirement.

Budget and appropriation controls in the departments may be insufficient to avoid overspending and waste.

Municipal policymakers may have deliberately understated expenditure requirements in the first place. Such practices usually result if policymakers bow to political pressures to expand programs without increasing revenues.

The municipality also may have fallen victim to a series of emergencies which require special expenditures. (Model budgetary practices are described in **An Operating Budget Handbook for Small Cities and Other Governmental Units**.)

TREND TWELVE

Rapid Increases in Employee Fringe Benefits

This trend is measured by comparing the yearly total fringe benefit cost per municipal employee for the past five years, measured as follows:

$$\frac{\text{TOTAL FRINGE BENEFIT COST}}{\text{NUMBER OF MUNICIPAL EMPLOYEES}}$$

Obtaining such a cost figure may not be easy since many local governments fail to quantify some costs such as vacation and sick leave, or to assemble all benefit costs in one place. Fringe benefit costs are often effectively hidden from the policymakers because they are not considered together at a single point in time.

Whether hidden or not, fringe benefits may be increased, but they seldom are reduced. Rapidly growing fringe benefit costs represent a trend which will carry over into future years, thus placing demands on future revenues and reducing financial flexibility. It is another way to lose future financial independence through heavy obligations to employees. If this trend is found, you should make a careful examination of its implications.

TREND THIRTEEN

Rates for Key Revenue Sources Are Approaching Legal Ceilings

The rates which towns and cities may charge for their various taxes and fees are sometimes limited by state laws or municipal charter provisions. Limitations on the property tax rate, for example, typically have wide appeal to taxpayers. Such limitations constrain the flexibility of the municipality and can restrict its financial independence when tax and fee rates reach these legal limits. The trend is measured by computing the ratio of the actual rates to legal limits as follows:

$$\frac{\text{LEGAL RATE}}{\text{ACTUAL CURRENT RATE}}$$

This ratio should be computed for each revenue source where a legal limit beyond municipal control has been established.

A ratio approaching one indicates that the financial flexibility of the revenue source in question may be endangered. Actions which your municipality may take to avoid this difficulty include:

- attempting to remove the legal restriction;

- encouraging growth in the revenue base so that rates would not have to be increased to increase revenues; and,

- diversification of revenue sources to reduce pressure on those sources where limits apply.

TREND FOURTEEN
Growing Proportion of Municipal Expenditures Made to Fund Mandated Costs

Mandated costs are expenditures which a town or city must make to comply with specific legal requirements of a higher level of government (usually the state government). This trend is computed by comparing mandated costs to total municipal expenditures as follows:

$$\frac{\textbf{MANDATED COSTS}}{\textbf{TOTAL EXPENDITURES}}$$

A growing ratio indicates that mandated costs are assuming a greater role in municipal finances. Since mandated costs are beyond municipal control, their growth threatens to reduce financial flexibility.

CHAPTER THREE
Municipal Productivity Declining

In this day of resource scarcities and growing labor costs, it is vital that municipal governments, like their counterparts in the private sector, continuously attempt to provide more and better services at less cost. This goal can only be achieved through steady improvement in the productivity of municipal operations. The alternative is a growing tax burden on municipal residents which ultimately may drive business and residents out of the city.

Municipal productivity is not an easy factor to measure because many of the services and benefits which towns and cities provide are intangible. The following trends are generally useful in measuring municipal productivity.

- Number of municipal employees per capita increasing. *(15)*

- Municipal expenditures per capita after adjustments for inflation increasing. *(16)*

- Municipal enterprises incurring operating losses. *(17)*

- Customer rates for municipal enterprises rising rapidly. *(18)*

If most of these trends are found, your municipality should consider implementing productivity improvement programs immediately. Such programs might aim at:

- improving work methods;

- using better or labor saving technology in municipal operations;

- enhancing employee skills;

- increasing employee motivation; and,

- establishing better organization and management.

Trends *(15)* - *(18)* are described more fully in the following yellow pages.

TREND FIFTEEN

Number of Municipal Employees Per Capita Increasing

This trend is measured by dividing the total number of municipal employees by city population for each of the last five years as follows:

TOTAL NUMBER OF MUNICIPAL EMPLOYEES
MUNICIPAL POPULATION

To refine your analysis, you might wish to develop a similar measure for each department or program (i.e., number of employees per capita by department or program).

This trend is a broad measure of municipal productivity if one assumes that the need for services is directly proportional to city population. Obviously, this assumption cannot be accepted without question in all cases. Consequently, if an increasing trend is found, further analysis would be needed to ascertain whether productivity is actually declining or if the citizens are simply demanding more labor intensive services.

TREND SIXTEEN

Municipal Expenditures Per Capita Increasing

This trend is measured by dividing municipal expenditures by city population over the past five years. If possible, expenditures should be adjusted by an inflation factor such as the Consumer Price Index (CPI). The computation would appear as follows:

MUNICIPAL EXPENDITURES ÷ CPI
MUNICIPAL POPULATION

Again, this measure might be refined by developing a separate indicator for each department or program.

As with the previous indicator, this is a broad measure of municipal productivity which requires further analysis to ascertain its meaning in each jurisdiction. An increasing trend could mean that municipal productivity is falling.

TREND SEVENTEEN

Municipal Enterprises Incurring Operating Losses

This trend is measured by assembling the net income from the operating statement for each municipal enterprise over the last five years. Consistent or growing losses may mean that:

- inflation in cost factors beyond the control of management have driven costs beyond revenue raising capabilities;

- rates are unreasonably low;

- demand for the services or goods supplied by the municipality is weak, and thus, sales volumes do not cover all costs; or,

- operations are inefficient.

Only the latter of these is a direct productivity problem. However, the severity of the other three problems might be reduced through improved productivity.

TREND EIGHTEEN

Rates Charged for Municipal Enterprises Are Increasing Rapidly

This trend is measured by comparing yearly municipal charges for enterprise fund services over the past five years. Rapidly growing rates could indicate that the productivity of the enterprise is not improving sufficiently to offset inflationary cost increases. An analysis should be made to determine if improved productivity is feasible.

CHAPTER FOUR

A Large Amount of Current Costs Are Being Deferred to the Future

It is always tempting, from the political perspective, to provide services and benefits today and pay for them later. Unfortunately, in the public sector, there are several relatively easy ways to do this.

All the cities which recently faced fiscal crises had indulged liberally in this practice. Deferral of current costs to the future can create an enormous, invisible burden on future local revenues.

The following trends should be closely watched to determine if an unreasonable level of cost is being deferred to the future.

- Short-term debt and other obligations outstanding at year end growing as a percent of total own source revenues. *(19)*

- Long-term debt being applied to operating programs. *(20)*

- Declining funding of capital items such as street repaving, new equipment, etc. *(21)*

- Increasing deferral of current pension costs. *(22)*

Any one of these trends can spell trouble in the future for your town or city. If several trends are found, your municipality could be headed for serious fiscal difficulty. Action should be taken to begin funding all costs currently by:

- eliminating the use of debt financing for operations;

- paying for pensions currently; and,

- replenishing or renewing the capital base of the municipality on a timely basis. (This may require the institution of a formal capital programming and budgeting process as described in **A Capital Improvements Programming Handbook for Small Cities and Other Governmental Units.**)

Trends *(19)* - *(22)* are described more fully in the following yellow pages.

TREND NINETEEN

Short-Term Debt Outstanding and Other Obligations at Year End Growing as a Percent of Total Own Source Revenues

This trend is measured by dividing the total amount of short-term debt outstanding at year end (including loans, notes payable, and unpaid vendor invoices) by the total amount of revenues collected for each of the five preceding years. The formula is as follows:

NOTES PAYABLE + ACCOUNTS PAYABLE + VOUCHERS PAYABLE
TOTAL OWN SOURCE REVENUES

An increasing trend here indicates that the municipality is spending beyond its means each year and rolling the cost forward into subsequent years. Such a practice was followed for many years by the cities which recently experienced fiscal crises.

TREND TWENTY

Long-Term Debt Being Applied to Operating Programs

This trend is measured by analyzing the uses to which bond proceeds are put. The use of long-term debt to fund current operations is an obviously direct transfer of current costs to a future period. If found, the practice should be stopped immediately. (The practice also may be illegal.)

TREND TWENTY-ONE

Capital Outlays as a Percent of Total City Expenditures Are Declining

This trend can be computed by dividing the total amount expended for capital items, including both capital projects and capital items purchased through the operating budget, by total local expenditures as follows:

CAPITAL OUTLAYS
TOTAL EXPENDITURES

A declining trend may have two alternate meanings:

- the capital base of the city or town has reached the optimum level and further enhancement is not needed; or,

- current capital needs are not being met so the capital infrastructure of the city may be deteriorating, creating a large requirement in the future for capital outlays.

Careful analysis of the municipality's capital needs would be required to ascertain if current capital costs are being deferred unreasonably.

TREND TWENTY-TWO
Deferral of Pension Liabilities

The trends to consider in the area of pensions are described below:

- unfunded pension liability per capita is increasing;

- unfunded pension liability as a percent of the assessed value of real estate is increasing;

- ratio of pension system assets to benefits paid is declining;

- ratio of annual pension system receipts to disbursements is declining; and,

- investment earnings on pension system assets as a percent of annual benefits paid is declining.

Negative results from any of these trends could mean that current pension costs are not being met and large future cost could be building. In-depth analysis of your pension program would be needed to fully assess potential problems.

CHAPTER FIVE
Use of Unsound Financial Management Practices

Sound financial management practices are important for many reasons. Sound financial management practices can help a town or city withstand the difficulties which arise from an eroding economic base. In addition, through sound financial management practices, the kinds of information local government needs to evaluate its fiscal posture and avoid fiscal problems can be produced routinely. Conversely, poor financial management may hide a deteriorating fiscal condition from elected officials and/or the public. Finally, financial management is a factor which is under direct management control. Thus, its problems may be easier to solve than those in the other four major factors discussed. There is no acceptable justification for maintaining inadequate financial management practices. (Model financial management practices for smaller municipalities are described in **A Guidebook to Improved Financial Management for Small Cities and Other Governmental Units**.)

The following trends may indicate that your municipality's financial practices are inadequate.

- A steady pattern of budget overruns in specific programs or departments. *(11)*

- Real estate assessments vary significantly from true market value (caution: the real estate assessment function may be beyond your municipality's control). *(23)*

- Earnings on short-term investments declining. *(24)*

- Interest cost of short-term loans increasing. *(25)*

- Incidence of estimated/actual revenue shortfalls increasing. *(26)*

- Amount of taxes and fees uncollected at year end increasing. *(27)*

- Consistent failure to obtain an unqualified opinion on financial statements from the independent auditor. *(28)*

Any of these trends may cause problems, but if several are found, your financial management practices probably have some deficiencies. Action should be taken to improve the financial management functions of budgeting, accounting, debt and cash (or treasury) management.

Trends *(23)* - *(28)* are described more fully in the following yellow pages. Trend *(11)* is described in the preceding yellow pages related to the factor *Financial Independence and Flexibility Is Being Lost.*

Real Estate Assessments Vary Significantly from True Market Values

This can be analyzed by comparing the selling price of a sample of selected properties in the community to the assessed market value* at the time of sale and computing an average variance for the sample. The average variance could be computed for each of the last five years. Information on property selling prices should be available in Register of Deeds records. The following formula would be used for each property:

$$\frac{\text{ASSESSED VALUE} \div \text{ASSESSMENT RATIO}}{\text{SELLING PRICE}}$$

If the average of these computations in each year is decreasing, then assessments are lagging behind market values. Such a condition not only puts pressure on local officials to raise the real property tax rate, but also leads to taxpayer dissatisfaction because some properties may be assessed at a level which is much closer to market values than others. More sophisticated assessment procedures and more timely reassessments should be implemented to correct the problem.

If your municipality controls or performs its own assessment function, then direct action can be taken. If the assessment function is under the control of another organization (such as the county or state government), the municipality should lobby to have the improvements implemented at that level.

* Assessed market value is equal to the assessed value of a property divided by the assessment ratio.

TREND TWENTY-FOUR

Earnings on Short-Term Investments Declining

The trend is computed for each of the previous five years as follows:

$$\frac{\text{SHORT-TERM INVESTMENT INCOME}}{\text{TOTAL OWN SOURCE REVENUE}}$$

A declining trend may result from several factors:

- an overall decline in short-term interest rates has reduced the opportunity to earn investment income;

- cash management and investment procedures are inadequate resulting in small amounts of (or no) cash being invested at too low a yield; and,

- the municipality is operating on an ever-slimmer cash margin making less money available to invest.

While the first of these causes is beyond municipal control, the latter two are not. Action to establish an effective cash management program by tightening control on cash receipts and disbursements, by making reliable future projections of cash availability, and by investing available cash at favorable rates of return could be implemented to improve interest earnings. (See **A Treasury Management Handbook for Small Cities and Other Governmental Units.**)

TREND TWENTY-FIVE

Interest Cost of Short-Term Loans Increasing as a Percent of Total Own Source Revenue

This trend is computed by dividing the interest cost of short-term loans (and perhaps the cost of discounts lost due to late vendor payments) by total own source revenues for each of the last five years as follows:

$$\frac{\text{SHORT-TERM INTEREST COSTS (+ DISCOUNTS LOST)}}{\text{TOTAL OWN SOURCE REVENUES}}$$

An increasing trend could mean that short-term interest rates have steadily risen over the trend period. It may also mean that the municipality's cash management program require improvement to reduce the need to borrow or to delay vendor payments to satisfy current cash needs.

TREND TWENTY-SIX

Incidence of Revenue Shortfalls Increasing

This trend can be measured by computing the following formula for the past five years:

$$\frac{\text{ACTUAL REVENUE}}{\text{ESTIMATED REVENUE}}$$

A ratio less than one could indicate that the techniques for revenue estimation used by the municipality are not reliable.

It also could indicate that the estimates were deliberately high to make the municipal budget appear balanced. The jurisdiction may be overestimating other revenues to hold the property tax down for political reasons. If revenue estimates have been too high and they are used to establish spending ceilings, the municipality may be in danger of incurring operating deficits. Deliberate overestimation of revenues is an extremely dangerous sign because it suggests that policymakers are not willing to live within their municipality's financial constraints.

TREND TWENTY-SEVEN

Amount of Uncollected Taxes and Fees at Year End Increasing

This trend is measured by dividing the amount of taxes and fees billed or receivable but uncollected at year end for each of the last five years by the total amount levied or billed. The computation would appear as follows:

$$\frac{\text{TOTAL TAXES OR FEES RECEIVABLE AT YEAR END}}{\text{TOTAL AMOUNT LEVIED OR BILLED FOR YEAR}}$$

The percentage may be high or growing for several reasons:

- penalties for delinquencies are not sufficiently high;

- follow-up procedures for delinquent bills are inadequate; or,

- poor economic conditions are making it difficult for some taxpayers to pay their bills.

Each cause suggests a different response and requires a different financial management procedure to change the trend. The municipality should devote more attention to its accounts receivable function.

TREND TWENTY-EIGHT

Consistent Failure to Obtain an Unqualified Opinion on Financial Statements from the Independent Auditor

This trend can be determined by examining the auditor's report for the last several years. The auditor is supposed to give a fair and impartial review of the data presented in financial statements. This review encompasses an analysis of financial records, procedures, and controls. A qualified opinion may mean that certain financial practices or records are inadequate. You should review the underlying causes for the qualification to gain better insight into the problem.

Moreover, if your independent auditor is a Certified Public Accountant, the municipality should be provided with a management letter which identifies the strengths of current financial practices and points out areas where improvements are needed. Suggestions for improving the efficiency and effectiveness of your financial management process as well as the internal control of accounting operations should be included. Such a letter need not emphasize the negative aspects of the city's financial management, but it should set out a positive program for improvement where necessary.

In addition, a CPA should be capable of performing a review of administrative functions such as payroll and personnel, purchasing, data processing, and budgeting. Such reviews are not normally included in the basic audit responsibility. Good audit procedures frequently will touch upon these functions, however. It is, therefore, logical to build upon the audit to perform a more comprehensive administrative review. These additional analyses will help you identify how broader management practices which impact financial management can be improved.

PART II

Procedures for Developing and Maintaining the Trends

The trends just described can be developed and analyzed on a regular basis. The process would include the following steps:

- Assemble the data needed to compute the indicators.

- Calculate the indicators for each of several (at least five) prior years.

- Identify significant trends and assess the underlying causes of those trends.

These steps are discussed in the following sections.

STEP ONE

Assemble Data

To compute the trends described in Part I, a number of information elements would be needed. These elements may be classified into five broad categories:

- GENERAL ACCOUNTING ELEMENTS

- EXPENDITURE ELEMENTS

- REVENUE ELEMENTS

- PENSION SYSTEM ELEMENTS, and,

- STATISTICAL ELEMENTS.

The data needed for the information elements can be assembled into worksheets such as that shown in Exhibit 1. The elements comprising each category are described below. A letter and number have been assigned to each element for easy identification purposes.

General Accounting Elements

These information elements include those which should be obtained from the town, or city's financial statements and/or from its general accounting records. Listed below are the elements along with the most likely source of the information. If the data needed for these elements cannot be obtained from your jurisdiction's financial statements and accounting records, improvements in the accounting practices in your municipality may be necessary.

EXHIBIT 1
Sample Financial Data Worksheet

REVENUE ELEMENTS	19 ___	19 ___	19 ___	19 ___	19 ___
R.1 Total Assessed Value of Real Property	$100M	$110M	$120M	$130M	$135M
R.2 Assessment Ratio	50%	50%	50%	50%	50%
R.3 Estimated Revenue (by source)					
R.4 Actual Revenue (by source)					
R.5 Number of Building Permits Issued					
R.6 Number of Business Licenses Issued					
R.7 Sales Tax Rate					

G.1 Municipal Enterprise Income (for each separate enterprise). Drawn from the Income Statement for each enterprise.

G.2 Municipal Enterprise Rates. Can be determined by examining the ordinance or action establishing rates, or a rate schedule.

G.3 Notes Payable Outstanding at Year End for Each Municipal Fund. Obtained from balance sheets for each municipal fund.

G.4 Accounts Payable Outstanding at Year End for Each Municipal Fund. Same as G.3.

G.5 Vouchers Payable (unpaid vendor invoices) at Year End. May be on balance sheet, but may have to be obtained by a special procedure of adding up the value of invoices on hand at year end.

G.6 Taxes and Fees Levied or Billed During Year. Drawn from general accounting records for each appropriate tax or fee (NOTE: some taxes and fees are not billed in advance of collection, so no bill amount is available).

G.7 Taxes Receivable. Obtain from balance sheet for appropriate municipal fund.

G.8 Long-Term General Obligation Debt Outstanding. Obtain from long-term debt schedules.

G.9 Amount of Vendor Discounts Lost. Obtain from general accounting memorandum records or operating (income) statement for each municipal fund.

G.10 Legal Revenue Rate Ceilings. Analyze state laws, municipal charter.

G.11 Current Revenue Rates. Analyze municipal ordinances, rate schedules.

Expenditure Elements

The expenditure elements are those which are based on the expenditure of municipal funds. Some of the elements can be obtained directly from municipal financial records. Others may have to be obtained through an analysis of financial records. The elements are described below.

E.1 Total Municipal Expenditures. This element should be reported on annual financial statements. For refinement purposes, it will probably be desirable to obtain a separate figure for each major fund or fund group.

E.2 Expenditures by Function, Department, or Program. This element should be obtained from the annual financial statements. A separate figure should be obtained for each expenditure category.

E.3 Expenditures for Capital Outlays. Some municipalities summarize the total expenditures of the municipality by character in the annual financial statements. Character would differentiate among operating expenses, capital outlays, and debt service. If your municipality follows this practice, the amount expended for capital outlays in each fund can easily be obtained. Otherwise, you will have to analyze expenditure accounts to assemble the figure. The sum might include amounts expended for land, construction or renewal, and equipment.

E.4 Expenditures to Match Grants. You probably will have to analyze each grant program to obtain this figure.

E.5 Expenditures on Categorical Grant Programs. Determination of this data requires both judgment and analysis. First, a subjective judgment must be made as to what constitutes a categorical grant. These usually include grants which are dedicated to narrow purposes, and approved on a project by project rather than entitlement basis. Law Enforcement Assistance Administration (LEAA) grants are an example of categorical grants. Second, an analysis of expenditure accounts to determine how much is expended on such grants must be made.

E.6 Expenditures on Basic Services. Like E.5, this element requires judgment and analysis. A subjective judgment regarding what constitutes a basic service must be made followed by a careful analysis to ascertain how much is expended on those services.

E.7 Debt Service Payments. Follow a similar procedure to that for element E.3.

E.8 Original Expenditure Budget. This figure is needed for each function, department, or program. It should be available in the budget ordinance or budget document enacted by the legislative body of the municipality at the beginning of each fiscal year.

E.9 Short-Term Interest Costs. The figure should be a line item in the operating statement for each fund.

E.10 Mandated Costs. This element is determined by examining the legal provisions associated with municipal services and determining which costs are required by state and federal law. Obviously, a careful analysis will be needed to obtain this figure.

Revenue Elements

The revenue elements include all those which relate to the amount of funds billed and collected by the municipality.

Two elements must be obtained from the real estate tax assessor:

R.1 Assessed Value of Real Property; and

R.2 The Real Estate Tax Assessment Ratio.

In some jurisdictions, assessment ratios may vary among the different classes of property. For example, commercial properties may be assessed at 50 percent of fair market value and residential properties at 40 percent. In these cases, you will need to determine assessed values (R.1) by the property classes corresponding to these different assessment ratios.

Several other elements should be obtained from the annual financial statements. These include:

R.3 Estimated Revenue by Revenue Source; and

R.4 Revenue Collections by Source.

Finally, three elements should be obtained from general accounting records:

R.5 The Number of Building Permits Issued;

R.6 The Number of Business Licenses Issued; and

R.7 The Sales Tax Rate.

R.8 Short-Term Investment Income.

Pension Elements

The pension elements must be obtained from an analysis of financial records of the pension system(s) maintained by your town or city as follows:

P.1 Unfunded Pension Liability. Requires an actuarial calculation.

P.2 Pension System Assets. Obtain from balance sheet of the pension system.

P.3 Total Pension Benefits Paid. Obtain from operating statement.

P.4 Cash Revenues of Pension System. Obtain from financial statement by computing revenues earned less change in amount of revenues receivable.

P.5 Cash Payments from Pension System. Obtain from financial statements by computing accrued expenses less the change in amounts payable.

P.6 Investment Income. Obtain from financial statement.

Statistical Elements

The data for the statistical elements cannot usually be drawn from financial records or reports of the municipality.

S.1 Municipal Population.

S.2 Municipal Per Capita Income.

S.3 The Consumer Price Index.

S.4 The Number of Municipal Employees, and,

S.5 Total Fringe Benefit Costs (See *Trend (12)*).

The first three should be available from the local, regional, or state planning agency. A local bank or economic development agency might also have the data. Element S.4 should be available from the municipal finance officer or personnel officer. The local budget might also contain that information. The latter measure will be very difficult to assemble because it requires extensive analysis and subjective judgment.

STEP TWO
Calculate Trends

The next step in the analysis of the financial trends is to calculate the trends identified in Part I using the data elements just described. All the trends described can be computed from the information elements listed in Step One. The specific formulas, using the reference numbers assigned in Step One, are presented in Exhibit 2.

EXHIBIT 2
Calculation Formulas for the Trends

This exhibit presents formulas for each indicator presented in Part I using the information elements presented in Step One. Where possible, the indicators should be computed for each of the last five years.

TREND	FORMULA
(1) Appraised Value of Real Estate Per Capita Declining	$\dfrac{R.1 + R.2}{S.1}$
(2) Number and Value of Building Permits Declining	R.5; and R.4 (Building Permits)
(3) Slowing Growth or Decline in the Number and Value of Business Licenses	R.6; and R.4 (Business Licenses)
(4) Slowing Growth or Decline in Retail Sales	$\dfrac{R.4 \text{ (Sales Tax)}}{R.7}$
(5) Expenditures for Police and Social Services Increasing as a Percent of Total Expenditures	$\dfrac{E.2 \text{ (Police)} + E.2 \text{ (Social Services)}}{E.1}$
(6) Total Population Declining	S.1
(7) Income Per Capita Declining	$\dfrac{S.2}{S.3}$
(8) Growing Percentage of Expenditures for Basic Services Funded from Intergovernmental Grant Funds	$\dfrac{E.5}{E.6}$
(9) Growing Proportion of Own Source Revenues Committed to Meet Matching Requirements	$\dfrac{E.4}{R.4 \text{ (own source)}}$
(10) Growing Debt Burden	$\dfrac{G.8}{R.1 \text{ or } \frac{R.1}{R.2}}$ and $\dfrac{G.8}{S.1}$ and $\dfrac{E.7}{R.4}$
(11) Steady Pattern of Budget Overruns in Specific Programs or Departments	$\dfrac{E.2}{E.8}$ (for each program, department, or function)
(12) Rapid Increases in Employee Fringe Benefits	$\dfrac{S.5}{S.4}$
(13) Rates For Key Revenue Sources Are Approaching Legal Ceilings	$\dfrac{G.10}{G.11}$ For each revenue source to which a ceiling is applicable.
(14) Growing Proportion of Municipal Expenditures Made to Fund Mandated Costs	$\dfrac{E.10}{E.1}$
(15) Number of Municipal Employees Per Capita Increasing	$\dfrac{S.4}{S.1}$

TREND	FORMULA
(16) Municipal Expenditures Per Capita Increasing	$$\frac{E.1 + S.3}{S.1}$$
(17) Municipal Enterprises Incurring Operating Losses	G.1
(18) Rates Charged for Municipal Enterprises Are Increasing Rapidly	$$\frac{G.2 \text{ (Annual Change)}}{G.2 \text{ Base Year}}$$
(19) Short-Term Debt Outstanding and Other Obligations at Year End Growing as a Percent of Own Source Revenues	$$\frac{G.3 + G.4 + G.5}{R.4}$$
(20) Long-Term Debt Being Applied to Operating Programs	**No Formula - Must result from analysis**
(21) Capital Outlays as a Percent of Total City Expenditures Are Declining	$$\frac{E.3}{E.1}$$
(22) Deferral of Pension Liabilities	a. $\dfrac{P.1}{S.1}$ b. $\dfrac{P.1}{R.1}$ c. $\dfrac{P.2}{P.3}$ d. $\dfrac{P.4}{P.5}$ e. $\dfrac{P.6}{P.3}$
(23) Real Estate Assessments Vary Significantly from True Market Values	**Analytical process**
(24) Earnings on Short-Term Investments Declining	$$\frac{R.8}{R.4 \text{ (own source)}}$$
(25) Interest Cost of Short-Term Loans Increasing as a Percent of Total Own Source Revenues	$$\frac{E.9 + G.9}{R.4 \text{ (own source)}}$$
(26) Incidence of Revenue Shortfalls Increasing	$$\frac{R.4 \text{ (each year)}}{R.3}$$
(27) Amount of Uncollected Taxes and Fees at Year End Increasing	$$\frac{G.7}{G.6}$$
(28) Consistent Failure to Obtain Unqualified Opinion on Financial Statements from Independent Auditor	**Analysis of Auditors' Report**

Identify the Trends and Assess Underlying Causes

The third step in the process is to identify any significant trends shown by the indicators and then to determine what the underlying causes are.

One good way to identify the trends is to prepare graphs showing each indicator's movement over the trend period. Exhibit 3 illustrates such a graph.

If potentially unfavorable trends are identified, underlying causes should then be ascertained. Remember, a trend which appears unfavorable on the surface may be harmless. You cannot know the real impact until a background analysis has been completed. The development of the indicator is not the end, but rather the beginning of the analysis.

This portion of the process is the most subjective of the steps to be completed and, therefore, requires the greatest degree of analytical skill. It is also the most important step because the results will indicate whether your municipality is heading for financial trouble.

To assist in performing the analysis of underlying causes, a checklist of the most likely causes associated with each indicator should be developed to guide the analysis. A brief checklist of possible causes for each trend was presented in Part I. This checklist can provide a starting point for the analysis. These checklists should be enlarged and/or elaborated upon to meet the situation in your own municipality.

In addition, careful attention should be given to the interrelationships which exist among the indicators. Keep in mind throughout the analysis that the objective is to determine if the unfavorable factors discussed in Part I of this handbook are present in your municipality. Thus, if several adverse trends in a particular group are found, their importance is likely to be more significant than if only one such trend is found.

EXHIBIT 3
Graphing a Financial Trend

Graph of Trend *(1)* : Appraised Value of Real Estate Per Capita

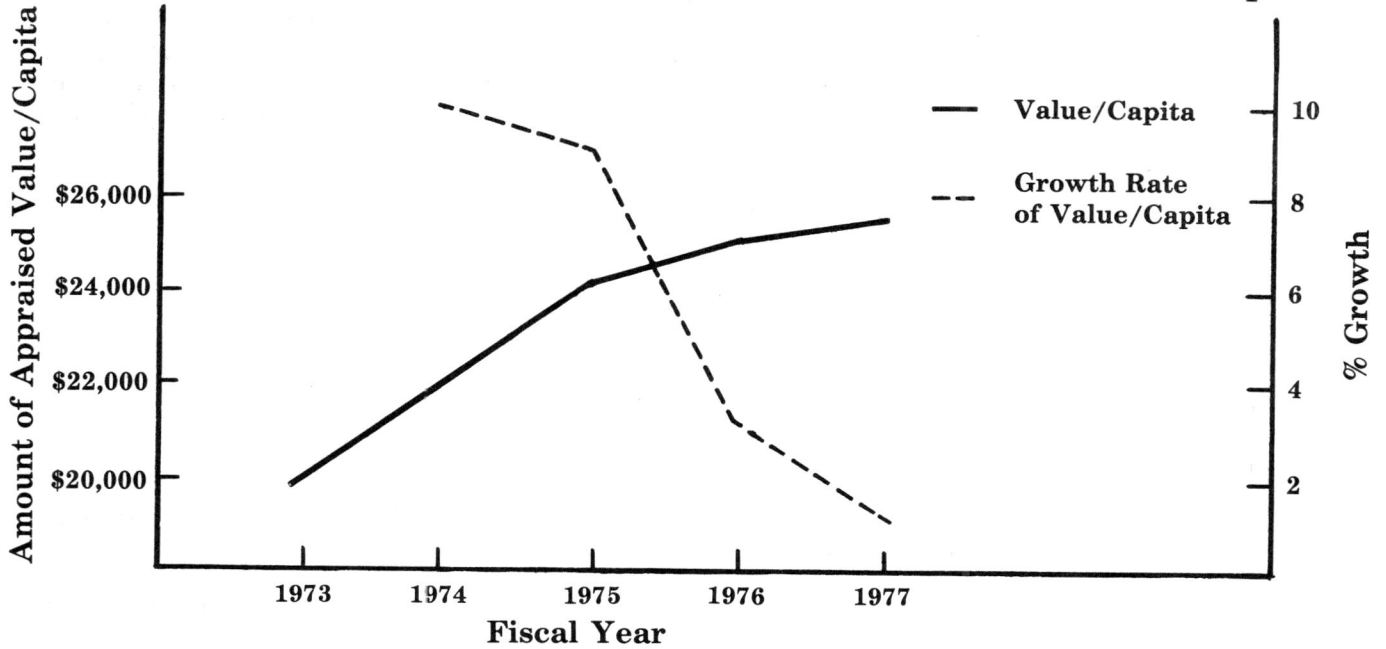

The above graph shows a significant decline in the growth of appraised values (from 10% from 1973 to 1974 to 1% from 1976 to 1977).

Continuous Maintenance and Analysis of the Indicators

The identification and analysis of significant financial trends should be made a regular annual process in your municipality. One individual (or group) should be assigned the task of accumulating the data, computing the indicators, and identifying the trends. That individual (or group) should also prepare an initial analysis of underlying causes. That initial analysis should then be carefully reviewed by other administrative and elected officials and enhanced where necessary. In a very small municipality, the independent auditor might logically be asked to perform the analysis. Larger jurisdictions might look to their own staff members such as:

- finance director;

- budget officer;

- internal audit staff;

- city manager; and/or,

- city planners.

In any case, those charged with the responsibility for conducting the analysis should exhibit an understanding of:

- the social, economic, and political factors at work in your municipality;

- the administrative structure of your municipal government; and,

- orderly methods of data analysis.

Establishing a formal ongoing responsibility for such analysis in a person or group will also help ensure that the analysis improves from year to year based on experience gained from prior years.

APPENDIX
GLOSSARY OF TERMS

Accounting System: The total set of records and procedures which are used to record, classify, and report information on the financial status and operations of an entity.

Accrual Basis of Accounting: The method of accounting under which revenues are recorded when they are earned (whether or not cash is received at that time) and expenditures are recorded when goods and services are received (whether cash disbursements are made at that time or not).

Activity: A specific and distinguishable unit of work or service performed.

Appropriation: An authorization made by the legislative body of a government which permits officials to incur obligations against and to make expenditures of governmental resources. Appropriations are usually made for fixed amounts and are typically granted for a one year period.

Appropriation Ordinance: The official enactment by the legislative body establishing the legal authority for officials to obligate and expend resources.

Assets: Property owned by a government which has monetary value.

Audit: A systematic examination of resource utilization concluding in a written report. It is a test of management's internal accounting controls and is intended to:
- ascertain whether financial statements fairly present financial position and results of operations;
- test whether transactions have been legally performed;
- identify areas for possible improvements in accounting practices and procedures;
- ascertain whether transactions have been recorded accurately and consistently; and,
- ascertain the stewardship of officials responsible for governmental resources.

Balance Sheet: A statement purporting to present the financial position of an entity by disclosing the value of its assets, liabilities, and equities as of a specified date.

Bond: A written promise to pay (debt) a specified sum of money (called principal or face value) at a specified future date (called the maturity date(s)) along with periodic interest paid at a specified percentage of the principal (interest rate). Bonds are typically used for long-term debt.

Bond Anticipation Notes: Short-term interest bearing notes issued in anticipation of bonds to be issued at a later date. The notes are retired from proceeds of the bond issue to which they are related.

Budget (Operating): A plan of financial operation embodying an estimate of proposed expenditures for a given period (typically a fiscal year) and the proposed means of financing them (revenue estimates). The term is also sometimes used to denote the officially approved expenditure ceilings under which a government and its departments operate.

Budget Calendar: The schedule of key dates or milestones which a government follows in the preparation and adoption of the budget.

Budget Document: The official written statement prepared by the budget office and supporting staff which presents the proposed budget to the legislative body.

Budget Message: A general discusssion of the proposed budget presented in writing as a part of or supplement to the budget document. The budget message explains principal budget issues against the background of financial experience in recent years and presents recommendations made by the chief executive and budget officer (if not the chief executive).

Capital Assests: Assets of significant value and having a useful life of several years. Capital assets are also called fixed assets.

Capital Budget: A plan of proposed capital expenditures and the means of financing them. The capital budget is usually enacted as part of the complete annual budget which includes both operating and capital outlays. The capital budget should be based on a capital improvement program (CIP).

Capital Improvement Program: A plan for capital expenditures to be incurred each year over a fixed period of several future years setting forth each capital project, identifying the expected beginning and ending date for each project, the amount to be expended in each year, and the method of financing those expenditures.

Capital Outlays: Expenditures for the acquisition of capital assets.

Capital Projects: Projects which purchase or construct capital assets. Typically a capital project encompasses a purchase of land and/or the construction of a building or facility.

Cash Basis: The method of accounting under which revenues are recorded when received in cash and expenditures are recorded when paid.

Cash Flow Budget (Cash Budget): A projection of the cash receipts and disbursements anticipated during a given time period. Typically, this projection covers a year and is broken down into separate projections for each month, week and/or day during the year.

Certificate of Deposit: A negotiable or non-negotiable receipt for monies deposited in a bank or other financial institution for a specified period for a specified rate of interest.

Cost Accounting: Accounting which assembles and records all costs incurred to carry out a particular activity or to deliver a particular service.

Debt Service: Payment of interest and repayment of principal to holders of a government's debt instruments.

Deficit: (1) The excess of an entity's liabilities over its assets (See Fund Balance). (2) The excess of expenditures or expenses over revenues during a single accounting period.

Demand Deposit: A deposit of monies where the monies are payable by the bank upon demand.

Depreciation: (1) Expiration in the service life of capital assets attributable to wear and tear, deterioration, action of the physical elements, inadequacy or obsolescence. (2) That portion of the cost of a capital asset which is charged as an expense during a particular period.

Encumbrances: Obligations in the form of purchase orders, contracts or salary commitments which are chargeable to an appropriation and for which a part of the appropriation is reserved. They cease to be encumbrances when paid or when an actual liability is set up.

Enterprise Fund Accounting: Accounting used for government operations that are financed and operated in a manner similar to business enterprises, and for which preparation of an income statement is desirable.

Expenditures: Where accounts are kept on the accrual or modified accrual basis of accounting, the cost of goods received or services rendered whether cash payments have been made or not. Where accounts are kept on a cash basis, expenditures are recognized only when the cash payments for the above purposes are made.

Float: The amount of money represented by checks outstanding and in the process of collection.

Full Faith and Credit: A pledge of the general taxing power of a government to repay debt obligations (typically used in reference to bonds).

Fund: An independent fiscal and accounting entity with a self-balancing set of accounts recording cash and/or other resources together with all related liabilities, obligations, reserves, and equities which are segregated for the purpose of carrying on specific activities or attaining certain objectives.

Fund Balance: The excess of an entity's assets over its liabilities.
A negative fund balance is sometimes called a *deficit*.

General Obligation Bonds: When a government pledges its full faith and credit to the repayment of the bonds it issues, then those bonds are general obligation (GO) bonds. Sometimes the term is also used to refer to bonds which are to be repaid from taxes and other general revenues.

Grant: A contribution of assets (usually cash) by one governmental unit or other organization to another. Typically, these contributions are made to local governments from the state and federal governments. Grants are usually made for specified purposes.

Internal Control: A plan of organization for purchasing, accounting, and other financial activities which, among other things, provides that:
- the duties of employees are subdivided so that no single employee handles a financial action from beginning to end;
- proper authorizations from specific responsible officials are obtained before key steps in the processing of a transaction are completed; and,
- records and procedures are arranged appropriately to facilitate effective control.

Internal Service Fund: (formerly called Intragovernmental Service Funds): Funds used to account for the financing of goods or services provided by one department or agency to other departments or agencies of a government, or to other governments, on a cost-reimbursement basis.

Investment: Securities and real estate purchased and held for the production of income in the form of interest, dividends, rentals or base payments.

Investment Instrument: The specific type of security which a government purchases and holds.

Liability: Debt or other legal obligations arising out of transactions in the past which must be liquidated, renewed or refunded at some future date. **NOTE:** The term does not include encumbrances.

Limited Liability Bonds: When a government issues bonds which do not pledge the full faith credit of the jurisdiction, it issues limited liability bonds. Typically, pledges are made to dedicate one specific revenue source to repay these bonds, or some other special repayment arrangements are made.

Liquidity (of investments): The ability to convert an investment to cash promptly with minimum risk to principal or accrued interest.

Maturities: The dates on which the principal or stated values of investments or debt obligations mature and may be reclaimed.

Object of Expenditure: Expenditure classifications based upon the types or categories of goods and services purchased. Typical objects of expenditure include:
- personal services (salaries and wages);
- contracted services (utilities, maintenance contracts, travel);
- supplies and materials; and,
- capital outlays.

Performance Measures: Specific quantitative measures of work performed within an activity or program (e.g., total miles of streets cleaned). Also, a specific quantitative measure of results obtained through a program or activity (e.g., reduced incidence of vandalism due to new street lighting program).

Purchase Order: A document issued to authorize a vendor or vendors to deliver specified merchandise or render a specified service for a stated estimated price. Outstanding purchase orders are called encumbrances.

Quarterly Expenditure Plan: The annual budget for a governmental activity can be subdivided into four three-month budgets, called quarterly expenditure plans. They can be used to monitor actual expenditures more closely and to identify problems more quickly than can be done with the annual budget.

Reserve: An account used to indicate that a portion of fund equity is legally restricted for a specific purpose or not available for appropriation and subsequent spending.

Reserve for Contingencies: A budgetary reserve set aside for emergencies or unforeseen expenditures not otherwise budgeted for.

Revenue: The term designates an increase to a fund's assets which:
- does increase a liability (e.g., proceeds from a loan);
- does represent a repayment of an expenditure already made;
- does represent a cancellation of certain liabilities; and
- does represent an increase in contributed capital.

Revenue Estimate: A formal estimate of how much revenue will be earned from a specific revenue source for some future period; typically, a future fiscal year.

Service of Objectives: The specific achievements which a government hopes to make through the provision of a service. The intended result of an activity.

Service Plan: The methods by which a government plans to achieve its service objectives. The service plan is the basis upon which the annual budget should be built.

Source of Revenue: Revenues are classified according to their source or point of origin.

Tax Anticipation Notes: Notes issued in anticipation of taxes which are retired usually from taxes collected.

Tax Rate Limit: The maximum legal rate at which a municipality may levy a tax. The limit may apply to taxes raised for a particular purpose or for general purposes.

Unit Cost: The cost required to produce a specific product or unit of service (e.g., the cost to purify one thousand gallons of water).

Voucher: written document which is evidence of the propriety of a particular transaction and typically indicates the amounts to be affected by the transaction.

Warrant: An order drawn by a municipal officer(s) directing the treasurer of the municipality to pay a specified amount to the bearer, either after the current or some future date.

Yield: The rate earned on an investment based on the price paid for the investment, the interest earned during the period held and the selling price or redemption value of the investment.